waterways books

After Rain

releasing new voices, revealing new perspectives

After Rain

waterways
www.waterways-publishing.com
an imprint of flipped eye publishing

First Edition
Copyright © Charlotte Ansell, 2008
Cover Image © Charlotte Ansell, 2008
Cover Design © flipped eye publishing, 2008

ISBN-10: 1-905233-09-4
ISBN-13: 978-1-905233-09-0

Editorial work for this book was supported by the Arts Council of England

Printed and Bound in the United Kingdom

Supported by
The National Lottery®
through Arts Council England

ARTS COUNCIL
ENGLAND

After Rain

Charlotte Ansell
2008

For Sean — co-creator of two poems infinitely more beautiful than anything I've ever written; Elsie-beth and Lily.

After Rain

Contents

How You See Things

In my home town,
the gravel on the driveway
doesn't stab my bare feet.
The dark is not absolute.
Stars are a multitude.

There is usually comfort in being
back where I grew up,
but now, in the background
of a photograph
on the wall, a piece of fruit
acquires a grotesque face.
The matches I picked up
in the restaurant display
a scallop shell with a tiny dagger
pointing up.
Except it looks like
an Elizabethan ruff,
knife towards the neck,
dripping blood.

It's a matter of how
you see things, analyzing
the signs; I could believe
the argument was nothing,
— I could just let it be —
but my heart sees danger
in everyday objects,
so I know this hurt isn't
ordinary.

No Certainties

When you left,
she said leaving is a process
not an act. Which made sense to me,
but didn't explain how
you could go so effortlessly — seamless.
You shut the door behind you

as if keeping it open would allow in
the possibility of your return. So, unwilling
to take chances, you said goodbye,
closed it firmly.
I didn't know then
how final your gesture would become.

I've lost count of the times
I've sat by the water
reflecting on its silence, like yours,
giving nothing away; remembering
the roses you gave me on Valentine's Day.
I kept the petals —

soft as your fingerprints on my skin.
Later I scattered them on the wash,
but these rituals haven't exorcised your ghost;
I still think I hear your footprints on the jetty
from the time you said,
I'll be back later, and never showed.

There are no certainties with people
like there are with the sea;

I like the water's loyalty, its absolutes —
people know to wear life jackets, to take ropes,
safety is measured, the dangers clear,
whereas your love was uncharted.
I dived straight in,
taking for granted that I could swim.

Swimming always felt like sex,
infinite, precarious, on the edge,
sinking into oblivion
until surfacing again to find
that nothing is ever completely washed away.
Your memory is a constant,
persistent as the tide, and I
always want to ask, *Why?*

I long for simplicity,
but there are no certainties with people
like there are with the sea;
those who recognise this are wise —
I know a man who only sleeps between tides,
whilst I still fall asleep at night,

dreaming of the seal that lives in these docks
the sound of seagulls,
foghorns from the Thames,
where the scum and muck
choke in endless highs and lows,
always coming back;

your remembered words
are like debris on the banks
of my mind - they should be lost

on the drift instead they return
endlessly.
I clutch regrets like stones,

heavy as I dive in
except I always seem
to float.
Thinking, *why will the water not hold me here?*
Why is it life begs to be lived
even without you?

Alchemy

Putting out the embers
of another charred and burnt out love,
bewildered, not understanding
the perfect sense it made.

Trying to figure out why you couldn't stay.
I ask all the wrong questions, you say.
Because reason has no part in this,
cannot access the reaches of your heart that

enabled you to start loving me,
then stop.
No amount of endless examination,
argument, recrimination,

of going over my mistakes
and yours,
could unravel the complicated formula
with the simple answer —

it wasn't to be.
So I can only wonder why
in this furnace
love couldn't be forged.

Why,
when we had all the raw materials,
we still couldn't make
gold.

Magician

He smiled and charmed me,
with his eyes sparkling and mine wide,
he drew coins from behind my ears,
made objects appear in my clenched fists,
knew which card I picked each time.

With a sly ease
he seduced my mind,
made me feel special,
captivated, blind.
It was my birthday,

I felt like a queen.
If it was sorcery,
my heart was his;
I can admit to being
unashamedly bewitched.

Lately, I had lost my spark.
Your withheld love
made me a pale imitation
of myself, faded grey,
but last night he found me,

coloured me in
and his best trick?
(Yeah he was good.)
He broke your spell,
finally someone who could.

That night everything
made us laugh too loud;

Pete, like a gangster
in his camel coat —
we thought we'd see

rows of watches
when he flung it wide;
Brian, flirting with the bouncers
to get inside, high on the music.
The staff handed out sweets,

I felt like a child, watching him
make a handkerchief vanish
without the use of his sleeves.
He enchanted me
with everything he did,

the club just part of his incantation,
painting our nails ultra violet
to shine in the dark. I spun round
drunk on his tricks,
the magic we'd found.

If this was courtship
I was a willing volunteer;
he could have thrown knives
or put me in a box,
I couldn't stop

the warmth
as the hairs on his arm brushed mine.
I was beguiled,
by this man who talked
of wanting to be hidden,

veiled behind his craft,
then took centre stage
whispered in my heart,
made excuses to touch —
it wouldn't have taken much.

But I didn't want reality
to burst the bubble
I didn't need to see
in order to believe, for one night
I wanted to be deceived.

Inevitably
the show had to end.
Petulantly I wanted him
to reveal the secrets of his sleight of hand
but I equally didn't —

wanted them kept concealed,
lest the charm be broken —
wanted his truth left unspoken.
As my night bus arrived,
I said a hasty goodbye

and watched him disappear.
I didn't feel cheated, we didn't
arrange another meeting.
I knew it wasn't real;
it wasn't romance,

but distraction I needed.

Five Senses

It's comforting listening to other people's lives,
like the television left on
in another room.
Sometimes I crave clean starched lines,
un-crumpled time.

There is peace in this world pared down
the horizons close,
the gauze of barbeque smoke
from the boats
moored on the other side.

The doors are open to late afternoon,
I sit and watch the dock, feel its calm;
the clouds enclose the water
snug as an eiderdown,
simplicity never lets me down.

My pace has slowed to a breath,
I am content
in ways only possible beyond regret,
able to forget the last trace of love,
it's sour taste.

Today, *alone* is the safest place,
touch a memory I've thought better of.
Sometimes I need no more,
than this sheet of sky
and the water outside my door.

Living in Our Dream

The first weekend in June:
it's doors wide open summer,
perfect boating weather,

the marshes on the bank
almost dusty in the haze,
the greener algae

we cut a swathe through
as the sun beats down his rays,
like a boisterous child

who hasn't learnt you can have
too much of a good thing.
Still we're not complaining,

letting the water carry
our no hurry, no worries, day along.
Under a bridge is an eerie message in red

'Murder Mystery: what killed Leroy
can be found in the shed.'
Is it a tip-off, a warning or confession?

Perhaps all three;
no one else seems to notice,
why would they? This is Hackney.

We are naïve, playing guitar
on the back deck with drinks,
vast smiles, soaking up the heat,

feeling the blessing this day has been,
so unsuspecting when some youths
pelt us with stones.

Mikey gets one smack in the nose.
Scarred and bleeding
later in the pub, he spouts

philosophy not revenge;
they were jealous, he says,
to their no hope eyes

imagine how we seem,
they just want to live in our dream.
I will never not be grateful,

for weekends amongst
the water lilies and reeds,
herons and signets,

terns, terrapins and weeds.
London's back garden
going to seed.

Graffiti the latest history,
banks of tyres stark and black as the water,
coots building nests from crisp packets and leaves,

but all glorious beauty.
The wild rose Masha
picks me from the bushes by the lock,

pulling up to the Anchor and Hope

where our madness pales besides
what spills from the doors.

A people kaleidoscope
thrown into the pot,
but miraculously getting on.

Maybe it's just too hot to fight.
Don't moor too close,
says a man, *there's a safe down there*

and the rest. You'll be stranded for the night.
Which sounds alright,
downing pints

in the still insistent sun.
We go on, up and beyond,
the river winding.

There's a boat here called
Widow Maker. I can understand why.
Further up it's cruel

that the boat with a high tide mark
of mud from the last time it sunk,
is called **Touch Wood.**

I don't need to.
I am as happy as I've ever been,
sharing food on the roof,

as the little one becomes first
a rabbit, then an aeroplane,
then a very sleepy boy.

It's been a long day,
so much enjoyed.

We Can Pretend

We can pretend it's not September,
that the evening's sharpness
is just some summer breeze.
I can argue I don't need your jumper,
like short sleeves would be fine.

We can make out it's an adventure,
not just going to the garage for fags,
that the chocolates you bought to cheer me up
actually tasted nice, didn't cost 99p for three,
and were really worth the thought,
even if you did grumble endlessly,
your generosity suddenly a bit too much
though it touched my heart.

We can convince ourselves we're happy
being single — not married or attached;
that we're nothing but pleased
for another friend pregnant, someone else
finding love, yet another recent birth.

We can act
like we don't need each other's friendship
quite as much as we do, that our bickering
isn't because we're lover substitutes.
We can be anything we damn well like;
as if the freedom of no-one to compromise for is nice
(which of course it is, sometimes).
We can make believe everything

and more — and with you I do.
So it doesn't hurt quite so much that he left.
I can even admit that I'm still in love
because I know fine well I am, however much
we laugh like nothing matters, take the piss.

The best thing is, I've always had you:
drier than deadpan,
cooler than chic,
with your inimitable style — so that
I never have to pretend at all,
just smile.

Tottenham Sunday

She's a Belfast girl in Tottenham,
via Africa, France, the Irish Sea.
She is stylish like no one else
does style — laughing at me.
A crooked grin, odd socks with holes,
scruffy tank tops, cut-off cords, boots
with clashing colours that somehow seem to go;
her wain on her arm snot nosed and rosy
cheeked — an angel child with his mother's
sense of mischief already blatant in his smile.

I'm on her doorstep in Tottenham
via Dalston Market, Stoke Newington cemetery,
the Buses on Stamford Hill.
It's a Tottenham Sunday —
I need nothing more today,
than to be here with this girl
and her child making me smile.
She is beautiful, hair grown longer,
the wee man bigger, frog slippers on
his feet, and we walk out along the back
alley with everything and nothing to say.

Fences mad with berries and rubbish,
a dismantled motorbike — like some slum town
in the sun; passion fruits with those impossible flowers
hang out over corrugated iron, all this mess
of weeds and plants, back doors spilling out
the noise of other people's Sunday afternoons,
the tunes from competing radios splashing

into the background traffic sounds
in a surround of contradictions.

We reach the canal — busy in September sun.
There's a woman putting nuts into crevices
in the trees for squirrels to find, there's
the drinkers by the lock: *Alright there girls?*
How's the boy? He's like a magnet to passers-by
as they peer into his sling trying to catch a glimpse
of his sleeping dreams, dimpled and calm.
I can't not love this town, the rubbish
next to nature is no fairytale to anyone's eyes,
but my view is not rose-tinted,
my eyes aren't blind.

There's beauty in the ugliness.
A family of swans glide over
the scum and shopping trolleys,
the deafening hum of cars over the bridge;
rotting flowers mark the spot of another's child's
death — we are quiet faced with tragedy
but the sun sets splendid over the rooftops,
every window blazing it back;
Tottenham glorious alive and warm,
as the lads share a joint on the steps, start
to style it out, look threatening, then move
to let us past. She just smiles,
tells her baby, look, this is where
you'll sneak your first cigarette,
this is where you'll play spin the bottle,
learn how to kiss, do all the things
your mammy did. All the while

we're talking — how could I need for anything
with a friend like this?

We get back to the house:
Daddy's making music
in an upstairs room,
composing tunes.
Mammy puts the dinner on.
Outside the sky is richest
blue, and through the branches
of a burnt and skeletal tree, a street lamp
shines like a baby moon.

Catching Up

Just chatting, giggling,
in this garden's dreaming
with the paving crooked, the stones uneven.
Cottage plants dance a riot round the back of the house
painted a seaside chalet blue.

We sit on upturned buckets,
the sun sinking low behind the trees,
jigsawing our lives together
since we've been friends.
Enjoying the craic,
the wine and fags; remember when
Cormac could first say our names,
when we climbed that scaffold
high above the Thames,
when Dave was ridiculed
for those tiny shorts he wore with pride,
the nights at Matt's, the kitchen reeling
with someone's fiddle, Ann on the bodhran,
Paul playing whistle, Matt in the middle
wearing a shirt louder than his smile.

Or last August
when your wedding crowned the year;
tears in my eyes, sharing the union
of you two and your boy.
Everyone with smiles wider than clowns,
feeling complete
the jazz competing with *diddly- ei*,
the folk tunes winning,
when Monica stood up, began singing,

and it seemed the whole world
stood still and listened.

We talk endlessly until we are numb with cold,
unable to get up and go inside for the warmth.
It makes me laugh
that the woman I never saw feared of anything
makes me go down the garden
to lock the gate in case of rats
so I, being wicked, scream and make her jump.

Finally it seems
even the night has had enough.
I come inside, the mosquitoes whine,
drawn to me, a beacon of heat
scribbling in the middle of the living room floor.
A whole pile of duvets to crawl into;
I feel like sleeping beauty, or the princess
with her pea. A Moroccan lantern
throws shadows of an entangled forest
across the walls, pools of light flicker
and fade. I am deliciously close to sleep.

I brush my teeth,
in the bathroom's beach
of sand pebbled walls, pussy willow
and blue
until I go to bed like I always do here
replete and full
with stories spun, with tales told
the delight in being friends,
in being loved,
of growing old together…
Yes, growing old.

Moni-ka-ka-ka

He says her name like *Moni-ka-ka-ka*,
breaking off from being an aeroplane.

She has a faraway smile again, moist eyes
dreaming of babies, fat ones, lots of them

pudgy arms reaching up for her, sticky
kisses and mouthing *Mmm Mmm* for Mummy;

tears that can only be quenched by her,
little ones she doesn't have to give back.

She was always the aspiring housewife,
glamorous hostess, sex kitten, skilled chef

a coffee table you'd be afraid
to put your feet on, banished stains, no mess.

She'd be a vision from the fifties
dutiful, bringing his slippers after work;

the man, the kids, the house in the suburbs,
lipstick flawless, no career but housework.

Impossible to see it in bed-sit land, room
heaped high, mountained junk, magazines

a small clearing on the bed where she sleeps,
mould growing on discarded plates and cups

and she'd be always out, flying, grooving
round any room, be-bopping up and down

bag slung on her back swinging, fag in hand
– the original festival party girl

but she would give up every all-nighter
hang up her whistle and her heels for good

forget the particular haze of dawn
hungry as birds, a chirpy afterglow

leave behind the sweet yeasty bread calling
from the bakery halfway up Brixton Hill

she would never swallow another pill
down a short, or re-apply her make-up

if it meant she could be the domestic
queen she carries close to her heart. Life

would be a perfect oasis of calm, waiting
for him to come home, a child on each arm.

Incidental Notes

Jazz at Pizza Express,
the first time in years.
Other memories whisper here
whilst the music lifts me
from the serious quiet
hovering over the candles.

Sat together
I remember loving him,
though I can't recall
the taste of his skin.
But the scent of him,
and the spark in his eyes remain.

Our legs brush. Accidentally?
Is anything?
I can picture that flat, the creaky bed
the rooftop chats, and the time on the stairs
when he would have left
but I kept him with *Please*.

I scribble, as I always do,
and he smokes his cigarettes in a relaxed way,
calmer these days.
Words define the space between us now,
the unspoken is safer, benign;
everything has changed.

The last piece of pizza lies on the plate
like a reproach. I forgave
a long time ago;
it's just good to see him again.
The past is simply that;
years have soaked up those tears.

The present is tense
with a slight electricity
that hasn't gone away.

Early Days

Your room like a child's, paint-box
primary, solid, comforting.

Up the ladder to the split
level, 'round the corner your bed
and the window wide
to the noisy lift of the breeze.

I am like a cat, exploring the space,
trying out corners, checking out the territory
from every angle. I don't know how
but every time I see you it's magical.
(though the tea you make tastes
like milk and dishwater.)

This house reminds me of Brixton
days, the bus Jen lived in one winter,
those summers spent lying
in the hammock in Rhymer Street
with her, surrounded by towers of sunflowers.
A house full of dreamers, the colours
rich, monsoon, someone always playing
tunes, easy days. Breaking into the Lido
after dark, swimming under the stars
swallowed by the ink of the water.
It all resonates here, with you. You are
what I know. I am happy balancing
on the step as you tell me the story
of Ariadne's thread, Theseus and the Minotaur,
you hum tunes as evening grows
and the shouts of children fade
to a mother calling them home.

It's like a spell, spun out,
precious, but my heart is
not easy, wound tight
like a spring, refusing to let go.

You ask me how I feel; I say
like a hedgehog, prickles ready.
You say you think you are
falling. I might begin to
believe you;

that's what I am afraid of.

But not very.

Unspoken Poetry

Each night I crave the warm cradle
which is the space
your body makes for mine.
Each night I wait
to fall asleep within your arms
and feel contained.

We have finally settled into love,
given up the struggle of our differences.
Your body's language belittles words;
you are not one for declaration.
It is in the silent details,
the loyalty of your being here,
that I feel stilled.

You give me flowers
but see more meaning
in bringing tools, chopping wood for the fire,
fixing what is broken.
Yours is the unspoken poetry
in cups of tea and smiles.

You have lived a lifetime in solidity,
mechanics and electricity.
You need concrete facts, things
that come with a manual, or rationale —
more comfortable with problems
you can solve with your hands and your brain.

I have lived forever
in the abstract, constructing a written world,
hiding behind words.

You say they are fickle,
not to be trusted, vulnerable to lies;
actions are the truth you set store by.

In my paper tower
poems litter the stairs
with no resonance here.

Perhaps this is why
I never could write you a love poem, never
tried to put a kiss on the page,
never tried to capture
the open book of your embrace.
Because love is not the frailty
of something said that fades.

It is not words on paper that hold
no faith. It is crawling
into your body's whispered comfort
each and every night, not fighting
belief, but trusting my quietened heart
— your closeness feels right.

River View

Tower Bridge glitters like a monstrous cake decoration above the Thames; implacable, brooding. Other lights, deceitful in the distance, seem fitting for our visit to this barge moored just past the shadow of the bridge. Even the boat is intimidating, stained glass in the windows throwing shards of colour across the walkways we negotiate, the wooden slats haphazard, so that even before we reach the door I feel the need for caution.

Dinner with your ex- and her new man, saying hello my eyes are alert for complication, aware of the ties, wondering where loyalty will fall, its lines. Wine and cigarettes — an inevitable politeness shimmers on the surface, but it would do with the tide still out, there is no depth. Only later will the riverbed be hidden beneath the rise and fall of waves. But perhaps all four of us feel the weight even this early on.

She is beautiful, huge luminous eyes; she shines and in my heart throbs a dull ache of second best. She is effusive, telling me how happy she is that we've met, that I'm lovely; she's glad because that's what you deserve but I can't quite trust her yet. The first push of the river coming in below sways the boat leaving me unsteady on my feet, wrong-footed by her ease. It's all innocent, without tension, and none of us allude to the strangeness.

In another place, in any other circumstance, I would like her. And I feel a fool for letting it be more tricky than it is. Funny that many times I've wanted to meet her, to compare notes. If only lovers brought references. But this is no time to talk, and if it was, would she succumb to some female solidarity and share frustrations with me, or would she remain yours? Some untangle-able knots of your history together I could never unravel without her *confidence*.

In our conversation ripples spread. A trip boat far out in the river goes by at speed, its wash faint by the time it reaches where we are, but perceptible. These currents do not pass me by, there is much to be read as she asks you to analyse his hands and he lays himself bare to your scrutiny, all of us curious as to what it means. The glances you share with her speak of the years you spent and I feel myself withdraw unable to prevent it. You look towards me smiling, eyebrows arched sensing the shift, but I'm already far away in my thoughts.

I watch her furtively, wondering why it ended. I seek clues like reading the sky to forecast the weather but I can't see, I am too close for perspective. I feel the tide advancing slow but relentless, covering the mud, its flood unyielding. Outside smoking a cigarette, a wrinkled reflection of London is lit ragged on the water. I draw into myself knowing this unease is all my own. You have done nothing wrong but words swirl around my head making me long for paper to jot my thoughts on.

Later we retrace out steps and I let go your hand to jump the platforms myself, to regain a little control. Then, riding pillion on your motorbike I practice not holding on to you. It feels safer. Separation marks the way home.

Tonight I will crawl into bed, into your waiting arms, you'll ask if I'm alright, and I'll pray that this divide can be navigated. But whatever is in the past and in my fears, I hold the possibility of our tomorrows that should be enough.

Faith

Is this
a beginning or an end, or both ?
The silence is companionable,
not empty,
with me scribbling poems,
you picking out tunes on your guitar;
what is happening isn't said.
We did analysis to death.

It's snug here by the stove
but the cigarette butts in the ashtray
look like bones.
The warmth is deceptive
as the fire destroys,
amongst these skeletons
it's unlikely
a phoenix will rise.

Like Ezekiel in the desert,
surrounded by bones
on the valley floor –
dry bones, until God asked
Can these bones live? and he replied
You alone know.
Will I too find faith,
or am I blind?

Last night
you kissed me.
The answers are not in your words.

You contradict yourself
more times than I draw breath,
but your eyes and smile suggest
a resurrection.
This isn't over yet.

Storm

There's a storm threatening; but there always was with you. The lightning flashes behind your head as we sit out in the bow of the boat, the water no longer calm, the sky made darker than evening by these clouds.

Our conversation feels as electric as the weather. I remember the storm in Alicante; I was restless all day then too. Not knowing why until flashes of brilliance spun all around us as we sat on the rooftop, an almost perfect circle of lightning's friction against the sky.

I was so often tense, fraught with uncertainty. You drank too much and I never knew when that anger — your paranoia — would flare up, or when it would die out again to quiet. We are older now, weathered by the years and I can no more go back than I can forward, no more sure now than I ever was. You charm me, you always did, but I keep silent and wait – cautious. Too early, too few days in your company again to take a risk, to wonder out loud what this might have been, or is.

I always loved a storm, the danger so apparent, so palpable. The water below us catches fractures of light from the moon, the surface broken by tiny waves, the black beneath merging seamlessly with the inky sky.

All evening I feel there is something I want to say but can't think what. We carry on talking, maintain a certain distance to buy safety. I do not ask if you also feel this, you don't ask me. Heavy in my mind is the imprint of the other night, when I was all too aware you hadn't changed as much as I had thought or hoped. But tonight we are easier with each other; it's our surroundings that are unsettled.

Later, you prepare to sleep in the back cabin. I watch you reach for the lamp from where I lie in a separate bed, with the divide no greater or lesser than our words. You call out to tell me that the storm has passed and I, aware of all your thunder, think perhaps it has — for now.

I Wrote This One For You

I wrote this one for you;
so you wouldn't feel humiliated,
hearing me read a poem
about a lover who was not you,
all that raw vulnerability spilling
into everyone's laps so they can
clap, whilst you hide away
scarred by my honesty.

So I wrote this one for you,
with all your fractured sensitivity,
putting your sunglasses on
because you know your eyes
say too much, and you don't
want to be read so easily,

when the stakes are this high.

I wrote this for you,
in memory of the songs you played
on your guitar to send me to sleep.
For the dance,
when you led me back unawares
into your heart,
not knowing that for you
it was as if I never left:

each fleeting time our paths crossed
these years we were apart,
you remembered exactly what I wore

when we met. This is
for when, lying in your bed
in the early morning pale, you opened the window

so the breeze would cool my back.

For this and every other small
remembering, I wrote this for you;
to know, where others have been
in and passed out of my heart,
you were always the one
who hurt me most, but loved me best.

Before You

On the day we discovered your existence
your daddy rode his bike
crazy along a maze of lanes,
outstripping cars
with a rush of exhilaration and speed;
on the motor-way
in single-hand combat with the wind,
me clinging on half-afraid,
but trusting him.

We meandered our way to the coast;
past gingerbread cottages,
village greens...
Arriving, we climbed the dunes,
puddled in shadows,
crossed small deep ponds
to reach the edge,
dipped our feet in where it was shallow,
collected shells and kissed.

We took comfort in cups of tea,
the celebratory sun,
with the wind
full of mischief, untamed.
Perhaps this is how you will be —
with the ocean
wild in your veins.
On the day we knew your life had begun,
we thought about you,

what we would call you,
who you would take after…
We took you to the water,
an expanse of sky,
let you take your fill,
so we might hope
in your life,
anything
would be possible.

Gym: January

Daylight cuts the floor, brilliant
and incandescent, making the fluorescent strips
seem suddenly dull, nicotine-stained, yellow.
I am miner-pale squinting, like my baby
waking in the night (emerging mole-like
into the violence of the bathroom light,
all screwed up face and clawed fingers grasping).

Winter: hibernated, mortified, blubbery,
hiding in the stale sweat-thick air.
Back of the aerobics class, thrown by
the first sunshine of the year, exposing all
hopes of taut flesh and clothes that fit
again as artificial and cheapened.

There are mirrors on both sides;
an exaggerated reminder that it is
inconceivable to start anew, all past
lives a blur. Not only my body that
will never revert, snap back
to the time before
I carried her.

Nursery

It feels like the last days of us,
last of the weighted comfort of her
little body asleep against me, last of her
world being Mummy then everything beyond.
Safe inside the castle of my arms;
my smile, her sun.

She is so very young, it is too soon
to hand her over to strangers. My last
chances to catch all her 'firsts', leak
like sand through clenched fists.
Will they respond as soon as she cries?
Will they monitor every sneeze or cough?

Will they love her as much as me?
Of course not, but I have to believe it
will be enough.

Even now I miss her when we aren't
touching, if she is too long in her buggy
or sitting on the floor. I have to scoop her
up, draw her close, smell her *Johnson's* hair
and milky breath before the world intrudes
again, pre-empting the slow ache of days apart,

when I have to give her up, let others care
for the single
most precious thing I ever had.

Lot's Wife

We used to play a game of not turning round;
walking along the cliffs, my dad miles away,
impossible to keep up with.
Don't look back, or you will become
a pillar of salt, like Lot's wife, mum would say.

I never noticed what lay behind,
never caught time in my fingers
until I found a photograph from years ago
where she looks so young.
Now he has trouble bending down.

In their pension years, all the fury
of my adolescence gone,
rows have lost their edge, tuned
to a background of bickering, familiar
as a carpet's well-worn threads, years

of treading the same old paths.
One day she asks what I will do
with her jewellery when she dies,
as if I might have given it some thought.
He gets more anxious in traffic

and, though not frail yet,
the day is approaching
when they will need me more.
At Christmas I drive them to the cinema;
he comes out from the film

with ice cream on his face —
my heart aches.
On Boxing Day, the last
remaining grandparent dies,
the generations settle and shift

as my cousin's kids scramble
over chairs into waiting laps.
Mum and my aunties
aren't formidable anymore,
they are grannies begging kisses.

If Lot's wife was guilty
of looking back with longing, I am too.
But my pillar will be made
of photographs, favourite songs,
remembered conversations.

Migration

I think I hate her now
but hate's too strong.
I am numb; ice held to a wound.
I tell myself I don't love her anymore.

Eighteen, the first time our paths forked:
Finally away from home, I felt her
homesickness in my belly like a stone,
as if it were mine.

Twenty nine: She says why
can't I be happy for her? As tears storm
down both our cheeks and we yell.
We're in Durham- the trees outside sickly

orange, unreal. Right
then, I could still feel,
because my mind wouldn't allow me to
grasp she would really go.

But it was there, the violent wrench of days ahead
her children not yet born, our lives stretched
twelve thousand miles apart. It would have been
Better if she had cut me, cleanly,

instead of tugging, like intestines
pulled to breaking point.

Being twins, no one ever differentiated us
I answered to her name more often than mine
'til at least the age of twenty five, we have
ridden a see-saw of sharing versus selfishness

dominance versus giving in,
hating versus loving too long
to let these knots unravel into indifferent miles
with more than oceans to wade across.

We turned thirty-five
today. This loss won't ever heal;
the cost is a life sentence.

Nana

I suppose I just thought
you would always be there,
would live to see a century
like your mother before you.

You were never daunted
your force of will like a hurricane,
you were brighter than sunshine
sharper than rain.

Strange to say that eighty seven is far too young.
It seems too soon for you to go,
other people saying, *Oh she did well.*
A good age, a good run. — they don't know.

I think of you
trying to carry everyone's bags,
never staying still, so hard
to get you to sit down.

I teased you often, but you took it well;
I just didn't think I'd see you go
not now, not yet, not until
you had seen your great grandchildren.

Not 'til I had seen you again
at least one more time.
You'd been here so long,
I suppose I never thought…

You were seemingly indestructible,
indomitable, with a fierce love,
a mother's instinct to protect your own.
A pride in all of us

that never faltered, keeping
our childhood pictures on the wall
however faded,
as we grew to adulthood.

Your garden always insane with colour
even in winter;
the table always heavy with food
sponge puddings, pies,
egg custard, roasts,

doing what you liked to do most —
feed us.
My memories are full
of being spoiled, stuffed
with all your toil of love.

Did you never tire of working so hard,
of giving so much?
Did your resolve never fail?
Didn't it ever seem too tough?
To the last you fought on.

I know there were times
when the path you walked
was worn with pain
but I am left

with this imprint of your life,

in these dull November days
of rainbows after rain,
there is always a life
that demands
to be lived to the full.

You were
never daunted,
your force of will like a hurricane.
You were brighter than sunshine,
sharper than rain.

My Grandmother's Bracelet

I find it in my jewellery box, buried deep;
my grandmother's bracelet, the stones
gleam luminous as if still wet, the sea
flooding up the beach like milk on honey —
Blue Anchor, Somerset.

The chalet that clung to the bank,
each year more eroded,
the stubborn scratch of grass, less.
The water collected in an enamel jug
from the pump across the way,
dusty beach balls, the pungency of salt,

seaweed, sweets and ice cream
from the wooden shop on stilts —
probably just a concrete foundation now.
But I remember the holiday when grandfather
looked for these stones,
each one chosen for her,

the colours like snakes,
shiny and dull all at once.
These were always her shades;
jade, amber, pale grey,
tea, cream,
a faded tiger-orange,

some of them like her teeth

(there was always something sharp
and fierce about her, underneath it all).
I must have been about five or six:
Gramps, what are you doing?

He was seeking the stones that he would
have polished and made into her bracelet,
keeping forever the shine of the sea,
an act of love, proof beyond
their reserve of things unsaid;
beyond me, beyond time.

Nesting

In the middle of the gunnel of the boat,
more turquoise than blue, a moorhen
vainly tries to build a nest, but all her eggs are
strewn along the edge, vulnerable, too cold.

That foolish bird sat statuesque, immovable
for more than a week, as if there might be
hope. We were cruel, laughing at her attempt
to coax her babies back from death.

I left my tears in the hospital chapel.
The nurse patted my arm and said
she couldn't find a heartbeat. A week
later — no blood — I understood what

no mother could ever, willingly, accept.

Isle of Dogs Afternoon

Home is a houseboat,
nestled uneasily between Canary Wharf,
the Brunswick Arms, and the Dome;
we don't bridge the gap.

My life is all maternity
afternoons in a no-work world.
The Thames bank— all dogs, school-holiday children
men with their backs tanned tough as leather —
lager, fags and this surprising weather are no antidotes
to apathy; jobs are unlikely
now the docks have become marinas
or sailing schools.

Some Muslim youths have got a bong up
on the wall, even the girl in a hijab takes a turn.
On the shingle beach below, exposed
now the tide is low, is a bath,
some traffic cones, countless
bottles scattered in the stones.

Over on the grass a lad is walking
his rabbit on a lead
(I have to look twice)
but it's nice now the day has cooled;
the rivulets of sweat coursing down
my arms and legs have dried.

Honeysuckle over the walls
belie the windows adorned
with Union Jacks, West Ham flags;

this is NF country, Isle of Dogs; daytime
TV inertia means an almost-calm presides.
Amongst the racist graffiti, a lamppost's missing
light; it occurs to me these flats
look more beautiful by night.

There's a grudging feeling of live and let live,
of paths that cross but don't touch,
lives lived in boxes, behind glass
folk who don't get out much.
Outside, the ships and boats that pass dance
with the tide whilst Greenwich is only a mile
across the river, but a latte-and-pastries
world apart. On this side the old guard are
cut off in more ways than one, by a tower;
immigration of the suits and salaries kind,
a sense of community gone.

In the window of an upstairs flat
the birds in a cage, twitter
with Frank Sinatra above
the musty aftertaste of old age.

There are buggies everywhere
as the other mothers and I
share knowing mummy smiles.
My baby found her feet today;
pleased as punch
she won't let them go.
She couldn't know yet
how little any of us belong.

The view is all industrial,
but the Thames glitters like a mirror-ball
and the sun is out and shining
on an Isle of Dogs afternoon.

London List Poem

To those who tried to get on the train
before the passengers got off,
to every bus driver who wouldn't stop,
to anyone who left their chewing gum behind
or put their feet on the seats
despite the signs;

for all the tube strikes
stop lights, leaves on the line,
lack of air conditioning
in summer time,
the taxi drivers who say
I'm not going there mate,

the first post which is always late,
the workman's sharp
intake of breath
when you ask the cost,
the road signs
that offer no help to the lost;

for the traffic wardens who make
minutes on a yellow line matter,
the mad drunk who singles you out
on the bus,
those who top up their Oyster Cards
during rush hour,

every driver who's cut up a cyclist
or shouted *lucky saddle* from their car

(you know who you are),
anyone who neglected to say *ta*
when someone held open the door,
or let them go first;

to all those who cursed,
when it was a genuine mistake,
or let the door swing
not checking who was behind,
all those who mind
smoking in an outdoor space,

every sign in the park
saying **keep off the grass**,
anyone who can't return a smile,
who talks loudly throughout the film
or leaves their mobile on,
even answers it and has a conversation;

to the shop assistants who look smug
when your credit card is refused,
or say *Oohh you look really good*
when clearly you don't,
the ones that have forgotten
the customer is always right,

the cash machines that are empty
the bars that are too full,
the bar staff who think
you're invisible,
anyone who puked on the floor
in the nightclub loos.

2.

To the city of dreamers,
piss heads and schemers,
city boys, couriers and cleaners,
social workers and shirkers,
beggars, call girls and office workers,
the night club goers and the early risers,

the graffiti artists, the market traders,
the spend-it-all-quick and the savers,
the sensible and the ravers,
the newsstand men, Big Issue sellers,
the bikers in leathers,
the windscreen washers out in all weathers;

for every religion under the sun,
the activists and the armchair politicians,
the dole-queuers, the rich and famous,
the repressed and the shameless,
the wannabes, the 'C' list celebrities,
the scammers and those with integrity,

all amid the clamour
which is this city's life,
the freelance and the nine to five,
the shift work and the skive,
the work all day party all night;
for the London that couldn't be any other way,

where everyone tries to board the train
before the passengers get off,
where the bus drivers don't stop...

Tears Speaking

She cries.
He asks, *What's the matter?*
She shrugs her shoulders,
cannot say.
Words feel insufficient, ill-defined
like ripples on the surface of a pool
where a stone might drop,
fall beyond.
He hasn't yet understood
but shouldn't try;
this is body wisdom,
he cannot reach the answers with his mind.

She cries.
He is afraid.
She must be unhappy,
she will leave him,
he cannot make her smile.
His inadequacy causes him to build walls,
a defence around his fear,
makes him cruel.
He feels the need
to scale the obstacles, be brave.
His hesitation will not calm
either of their souls.

She cries.
It is her tears speaking,
raining down replenishment
on a desert of love denied,

containing ancient legacies of healing,
as witches used them to bind
herbs for restorative spells,
tears are a whisper to draw close, closer still.
Revealing a heart not broken,
but breaking open,
in this moment,
intimacy can arrive.

She cries.
He is unaware of the gift she offers;
communication at this raw edge
is truth, if he could just
read the signs.
But he is human, it makes him doubtful, insecure.
he thinks he disappoints her,
that he's not good enough.
It will take courage, strength,
his spirit, all his being
to see she feels too much,
that she is simply overwhelmed by love.

She

She is slight, frail, pale and pretty
with this fragile quality
like an injured bird,
heartbeat like a bomb
ticking too loud.
But she doesn't open her mouth,
doesn't say a word, doesn't
want to answer questions,
doesn't want to say that
she is Kosovan;
she feels ashamed.

She says that people pity her,
or they are curious, or unkind.
Or they criticise.
Or they underestimate her
because she comes from a country that is lost.

The TV documentaries portray
Kosovans as peasants
begging their way along the tube.
Women with babies
pleading with those who avert their eyes,
or wiping windscreens at traffic lights;
resplendent rainbow of scarves and skirts
in the heat, trying to supplement their vouchers,
so they can eat.

But she seems above this;
she just wants to fit in.
She doesn't want people
to know where she is from,

can't show pride in her identity,
feels too afraid. Some boys
she knows like to beat up refugees:
Because they should go home innit?
She says, *None of us asked to be here.*
We didn't want to come.
She will admit to being Eastern
European, Polish perhaps, never Kosovan.

She wants to be seen as an individual.
She doesn't like her accent, feels inferior.
It would be nice if the English didn't
always ask: *Where are you from?*
Why are you here? Why don't you
go back now the war is done?
You feel you can hear beneath her wings,
a heartbeat like a bomb.

She's trying to appeal the decision to send her back,
cannot face what no longer feels like home, afraid
to find out if family members have gone. She
doesn't know where they are, if they are alive.
She says she has made a new start here,
has a new family: her foster carer,
her boyfriend and her friends.
But her carer is paid
until she's eighteen, hardly
a foundation where she can cling.

It's the little things;
like not being able to remember
the last time she was hugged,
needing her mum. With no one

making allowances now she's been here
so long, all she wants is to be accepted,
pursue her dreams and be allowed
to get on with the ordinary things.

She is slight, frail, pale and pretty,
with this fragile quality,
like an injured bird whose ribcage can't
contain a heartbeat this strong.
You feel sure though,
that she will not be beaten,
she will succeed, get on…

Brick Lane; all tribes are welcome

Brick Lane, no two faces the same,
streets that have always welcomed immigrants,
the signs in Bengali under the English names,
the Mosque that used to be a synagogue.

When people settled here
they brought wealth
in their disparity,
customs, foods and cloth.
The cockney blag of the market stall holder,
the weight of a small island in gold
around his neck:
16 double 'A' batteries a pannd,
Calvin Klein boxers a fiver for packs of three,
the Indians next to him with luxury throw-overs
— a tiger resplendent in grass,
but don't ask, don't assume
that what you'll get is what you see.

At the Beigel shop quality is assured;
the queue continually spills out the door,
hot salt beef, salmon and cream cheese,
coffee that doesn't cost a ridiculous amount.
I can't count how many accents swirl in the air
of misted breath, voices crying out their wares,
London as it's always been
arms open to many dreams,
people travelling many seas to come;
to be swallowed up and used?
The streets were never paved with gold,

the locals welcome not always warm,
sometimes hostile, sometimes aggrieved,
but weekend market bohemian chic
values all
and smiles at least are free.

Sunday morning peace
in the church of meeting lives,
not even a nail bomb
could shatter this compromise.
An Islam praise song mingles
with a baby girl's cries,
the waiters outside the curry houses
entice tourists in.
Further down in a café
Pakistani children in the window
eat ketchup and chips with satisfied grins.
Couples holding hands parade their mixed race love,
no one pretends its easy,
that it won't be tough,
but there's no problem here with inter-racial
if you look cool enough.

It's all about appearances,
the lad on the corner with knocked off tobacco,
says the coppers told him it's ok
as long as he's discreet,
and down the street
from the Jewish rag trade
to the Sun of Marrakech,
the Vibe bar and Ninety Three Feet East

rub shoulders with Bengali restaurants,
and the mess of bric-a-brac stalls,
where last year's rubbish
is someone else's prize;
whatever you want it's here,
whoever you are it's fine.
Communities are built on ties
of more than blood.

A Rasta calls out:
Aba Shanti,
dub roots and culture at Brixton Rec.
with flyers for Friday Feb the 6th.
A footnote says,
All tribes are welcome,
and I guess that's it.
Here at least amongst the young
and the beautiful from Brixton
to Brick Lane,
love knows no colour,
has no walls, dares to be free,
so often, almost by accident, here
there is a kind of unity.

Soham

A nation waits with bated breath; five days
since the girls were last seen
the newscaster said. Everywhere, talk
of what is front page news (as if
keeping them in mind will keep them safe)
no one speaks
of what they fear the most,
what they silently expect.

Then two freshly dug mounds
of earth discovered in the woods,
a jogger remembers he heard screams
on Sunday night, the strain all too visible
on the chief of police when morning reveals
itself more ashen than his face
he reports with barely concealed relief
that the investigation found nothing conclusive.

It's not them. A nation breathes
out, sleeps again. It's not them —
nor any other child this time.
Sometimes a large scale operation
uncovers other crimes, other children
who disappeared unmarked by TV
or Tabloid press — those unnamed.
We've heard it before; a police spokesman
said: *the body found in the Thames*
on Friday 12ᵗʰ is not that of missing schoolgirl…

The media has passed over countless
families whose grief was more private,
whose waiting never ends, whose tears
are unseen by a million watchers on screens.
100,000 children go missing in Britain
each year most return home within 72 hours.

Who sees? Who saw? Someone
should have asked those girls why
they were out; did their mothers know?
Someone should have told them
to go home.

Manchild

8:45 – another day in hell
as the bell signals
the end of registration.
He comes in late again, slouching

down the hall. Gets himself to class, opens
the door, ready for an earful: *You*
decided to grace us with your presence, eh?
What time d'you call this? 9B feels
honoured I'm sure. Don't backchat me
boy, don't even start. You're a disgrace,
you're an excuse, I've got
kids in here who want to learn,
kids worth ten of you.

The words stick, the words sink
in. No-one has asked him: *How are you*
doing today? Everything ok at home?
Of course they don't.

No, she turns the page, teaching him
the only lesson he's ever learned in this place;
to behave is to be overlooked.
Getting attention equals: you're in
trouble and you're no good.

So already at 9:55 the morning has angered
him. He is up and running through
the corridors, setting light to the bins,
kicking at the doors, swearing at the teachers
and then he's gone – trying to run
from every fucking thing.

Every night at home his mum is
drowning, the house just like a building
site – with cans and fag ends littering
the floor; the eviction notice came through
days before, she can't cope anymore
with his dad never there. When he is,

the man knocks them both around and calls
him *a worthless little shit*, says,
you ain't a man son.

The words stick. The words sink in;
as his dad goes, *come on then*,
staring with fury in his eyes
He tries to choke back tears of rage

because he's seen too much; seen his
dad touch his mum with no trace of love,
call her slut, seen him slam her against the wall
too many times, seen the blood trace lines down
her cheeks where no tears fall, her eyes blind
with alcohol, trying to fight against it all.

School is a getaway, but what's the point?
They just exclude him anyway.
They think he's trouble, doesn't know
how to behave, no discipline, no respect in him;
the way he is, is how he'll stay, is how he's always been
beyond help already – not yet fifteen.

But he carries on, thinking
he's got to try and save his mum.
In some mad way he feels responsible;
thinks if he weren't always messing

up and getting exclusion letters home
she might stop drinking; if he could
stop his dad from trying to kill her,

she might stop sinking. He's carrying
all this and more, all the time, shot
through to the core with helplessness,
frustration and despair – and, yeah,
what relevance are SATs and GCSEs,
and records of achievement when
he can't see a future?

He is a precious thing, a bright
bright star, incredible just to survive,
somehow managing to stay alive, a child
with so much potential. If only
his pain could be heard and soothed, if
only he was given the chance to prove
himself. But who is going to tell him?

Could he ever believe
something so alien to him?

The Demonstration

(Oct 8th, 2001)

Here is a heightened sense of colour
in the details. The police surround us
in a wall, jackets fluorescent, harsh.
The street lamps make yellow patterns
dance in the grass. The sky, pitched
midnight blue, the kind of sky you want
to sit under, count the stars,
let its depth edge your dreams.

The same sky which should comfort
like a blanket over the world. Instead
somewhere far off, Kabul, out of it
drop bombs
our government decided should fall.

The banners unfurl,
peace white, pale.
Writing red — as if etched
in blood. Something so good
in being amongst so many people
believing the same thing,
fighting for it with words:
Stop the war. No bombing.
But in the excitement
no-one is smiling.

You cannot help but think
where was the three-minute silence
for the Congo, Rwanda, Angola?
Does one life equal another,
or are some worth more than others?

Perhaps one voice is too quiet, too small.
What difference does it make
to demonstrate?
But if everyone thought
that, this crowd wouldn't exist.
If everyone had stayed at home,
who would resist the evil in their hands?
I thought my voice was too little,
but joined together with all of these
the noise becomes a multitude;

a roar, one huge voice
that cannot be ignored?
It's loud enough,
it's loud enough.
I hope to God, it's loud enough.

White Privilege

(with ideas taken from Peggy McIntosh's essay Working Paper 189. "White Privilege and Male Privilege" 1988)

Does talk of the race issue only
apply if you're black? Looking back,
I never had to think about it
but that doesn't mean I shouldn't think
beyond that tick box 'White UK'
for Equal Opportunities.

I was raised in a town where kids were
racist because no one told them not to be,
never saw anyone of another race until I was
five; when two African children came
to my school. We had a special assembly
to remind us to be nice to them,
to not treat them as different, as if drawing
attention to the fact wasn't treating them differently
anyway. They only stayed two days.

The population was white in our small market
town. At my secondary school there was one
Black family and two Chinese; I never had any
Black friends until I was eighteen and if you'd asked me
then I would have sworn I wasn't racist, wouldn't dream
of being. But, honestly, back then, I didn't really know

what it meant. I felt absolved from blame
because I meant no harm. It's easier,
if your house isn't made of glass, to throw
stones, to climb up ivory towers and look out below,
untouched and un-assailed.

But ask yourself, if your skin is pale;
when was the last time you tried to use a credit card
and were greeted with suspicion? The last time
the police stopped you for no apparent reason?

The last time you asked your children what
they did at school today and they said: *history
and civilisation*, but somehow your ancestors weren't mentioned,
had not been included with those who contributed
to make this culture what it is?

Did you stop to think that you were privileged?

I can be fairly sure that if I dress scruffy, swear
or shout abuse, turn up late, or am generally unreliable,
no one will think it attributable to the poverty,
illiteracy or immorality of *my* race. I'm not asked
to speak on behalf of *my* people
in some half-baked effort to be representational

It seems easy to infect this country with paranoia. But we are
all, in some way or other mixed — including the English.
Doesn't the hyphen between *Anglo* and *Saxon* testify to dual herit-
age?

Immigration is hardly new:

In 6,000 BC, Britain became an island, the first
settlers came; 410, the first invasions by Angles, Saxons,
Jutes and Frisians; 1581, London's population boasted
20,000 Africans. By 1630 the first South East Asians
were here; in World War II, 48 different countries joined

our fight; the Empire Windrush arrived in 1948 — so perhaps
the BNP are a little late, certainly misled, marching
through Bermondsey to 'Keep Britain White.'

Surely it should come as no surprise that
one in three Londoners come from other ethnic groups.
And if we needed any more proof — a couple more
facts: London was built by a Roman General who happened
to be black, and that flag — the white one
with the red cross proudly held aloft at football matches
in commemoration of St George, that true blue-blooded
Englishman? He was born in Palestine.

Oh, and was this climate ever really
hot enough for those three lions?

We Hope You Enjoyed Reading!
Let us know what you think by sending an e-mail to
editor@waterways-publishing.com

Thank You for buying *After Rain*. If you would like more information about waterways publishing, please join our mailing list online at **www.waterways-publishing.com**.

Visit our other imprints online:

mouthmark *(poetry)*
www.flippedeye.net/mouthmark

lubin & kleyner *(fiction)*
www.flippedeye.net/lubinandkleyner

flipped eye *(general)*
www.flippedeye.net

Lightning Source UK Ltd.
Milton Keynes UK
UKHW010719210321
380690UK00001B/37

9 781905 233090